Travel phrasebooks collection
«Everything Will B[...]

PHRASEBOOK

– ALBANIAN –

THE MOST IMPORTANT PHRASES

This phrasebook contains the most important phrases and questions for basic communication. Everything you need to survive overseas

By Andrey Taranov

T&P BOOKS

Phrasebook + 250-word dictionary

English-Albanian phrasebook & mini dictionary

By Andrey Taranov

The collection of "Everything Will Be Okay" travel phrasebooks published by T&P Books is designed for people traveling abroad for tourism and business. The phrasebooks contain what matters most - the essentials for basic communication. This is an indispensable set of phrases to "survive" while abroad.

You'll also find a mini dictionary with 250 useful words required for everyday communication - the names of months and days of the week, measurements, family members, and more.

Copyright © 2018 T&P Books Publishing

All rights reserved. No part of this book may be reproduced or utilized in any form or by any means, electronic or mechanical, including photocopying, recording or by information storage and retrieval system, without permission in writing from the publishers.

T&P Books Publishing
www.tpbooks.com

ISBN: 978-1-78767-148-5

This book is also available in E-book formats.
Please visit www.tpbooks.com or the major online bookstores.

FOREWORD

The collection of "Everything Will Be Okay" travel phrasebooks published by T&P Books is designed for people traveling abroad for tourism and business. The phrasebooks contain what matters most - the essentials for basic communication. This is an indispensable set of phrases to "survive" while abroad.

This phrasebook will help you in most cases where you need to ask something, get directions, find out how much something costs, etc. It can also resolve difficult communication situations where gestures just won't help.

This book contains a lot of phrases that have been grouped according to the most relevant topics. You'll also find a mini dictionary with useful words - numbers, time, calendar, colors...

Take "Everything Will Be Okay" phrasebook with you on the road and you'll have an irreplaceable traveling companion who will help you find your way out of any situation and teach you to not fear speaking with foreigners.

TABLE OF CONTENTS

T&P Books Publishing

PRONUNCIATION

T&P phonetic alphabet	Albanian example	English example
[a]	flas [flas]	shorter than in ask
[e], [ɛ]	melodi [mɛlodí]	absent, pet
[ə]	kërkoj [kərkój]	driver, teacher
[i]	pikë [píkə]	shorter than in feet
[o]	motor [motór]	pod, John
[u]	fuqi [fucí]	book
[y]	myshk [myʃk]	fuel, tuna
[b]	brakë [brákə]	baby, book
[c]	oqean [ocɛán]	Irish - ceist
[d]	adoptoj [adoptój]	day, doctor
[dz]	lexoj [lɛdzój]	beads, kids
[dʒ]	xham [dʒam]	joke, general
[ð]	dhomë [ðómə]	weather, together
[f]	i fortë [i fórtə]	face, food
[g]	bullgari [buɫgarí]	game, gold
[h]	jaht [jáht]	home, have
[j]	hyrje [hýrjɛ]	yes, New York
[ɟ]	zgjedh [zɟɛð]	geese
[k]	korik [korík]	clock, kiss
[l]	lëviz [ləvíz]	lace, people
[ɫ]	shkallë [ʃkáɫə]	feel
[m]	medalje [mɛdáljɛ]	magic, milk
[n]	klan [klan]	name, normal
[ɲ]	spanjoll [spaɲóɫ]	canyon, new
[ŋ]	trung [truŋ]	ring
[p]	polici [politsí]	pencil, private
[r]	i erët [i érət]	rice, radio
[ɾ]	groshë [gróʃə]	Spanish - pero
[s]	spital [spitál]	city, boss
[ʃ]	shes [ʃɛs]	machine, shark
[t]	tapet [tapét]	tourist, trip
[ts]	batica [batítsa]	cats, tsetse fly
[tʃ]	kaçube [katʃúbɛ]	church, French
[v]	javor [javór]	very, river
[z]	horizont [horizónt]	zebra, please
[ʒ]	kuzhinë [kuʒínə]	forge, pleasure
[θ]	përkthej [pərkθéj]	month, tooth

LIST OF ABBREVIATIONS

English abbreviations

ab.	-	about
adj	-	adjective
adv	-	adverb
anim.	-	animate
as adj	-	attributive noun used as adjective
e.g.	-	for example
etc.	-	et cetera
fam.	-	familiar
fem.	-	feminine
form.	-	formal
inanim.	-	inanimate
masc.	-	masculine
math	-	mathematics
mil.	-	military
n	-	noun
pl	-	plural
pron.	-	pronoun
sb	-	somebody
sing.	-	singular
sth	-	something
v aux	-	auxiliary verb
vi	-	intransitive verb
vi, vt	-	intransitive, transitive verb
vt	-	transitive verb

Albanian abbreviations

f	-	feminine noun
m	-	masculine noun
pl	-	plural

ALBANIAN PHRASEBOOK

This section contains important phrases that may come in handy in various real-life situations.
The phrasebook will help you ask for directions, clarify a price, buy tickets, and order food at a restaurant

T&P Books Publishing

PHRASEBOOK
CONTENTS

ks Publishing

Excuse me, ...	**Më falni, ...** [mə fálni, ...]
Hello.	**Përshëndetje.** [pərʃəndétjɛ]
Thank you.	**Faleminderit.** [falɛmindérit]
Good bye.	**Mirupafshim.** [mirupáfʃim]
Yes.	**Po.** [po]
No.	**Jo.** [jo]
I don't know.	**Nuk e di.** [nuk ɛ di]
Where? | Where to? | When?	**Ku? | Për ku? | Kur?** [ku? | pər ku? | kur?]
I need ...	**Më nevojitet ...** [mə nɛvojítɛt ...]
I want ...	**Dua ...** [dúa ...]
Do you have ...?	**Keni ...?** [kéni ...?]
Is there a ... here?	**A ka ... këtu?** [a ka ... kətú?]
May I ...?	**Mund të ...?** [mund tə ...?]
..., please (polite request)	**..., ju lutem** [...], [ju lútɛm]
I'm looking for ...	**Kërkoj ...** [kərkój ...]
the restroom	**tualet** [tualét]
an ATM	**bankomat** [bankomát]
a pharmacy (drugstore)	**farmaci** [farmatsí]
a hospital	**spital** [spitál]
the police station	**komisariat policie** [komisariát politsíɛ]
the subway	**metro** [mɛtró]

a taxi	**taksi**
	[táksi]
the train station	**stacion treni**
	[statsión trɛni]

My name is ...	**Më quajnë ...**
	[mə cúajnə ...]
What's your name?	**Si quheni?**
	[si cúhɛni?]
Could you please help me?	**Ju lutem, mund të ndihmoni?**
	[ju lútɛm], [mund tə ndihmóni?]
I've got a problem.	**Kam një problem.**
	[kam ɲə problém]
I don't feel well.	**Nuk ndihem mirë.**
	[nuk ndíhɛm mírə]
Call an ambulance!	**Thërrisni një ambulancë!**
	[θərísni ɲə ambulántsə!]
May I make a call?	**Mund të bëj një telefonatë?**
	[mund tə bəj ɲə tɛlɛfonátə?]

I'm sorry.	**Më vjen keq.**
	[mə vjɛn kɛc]
You're welcome.	**Ju lutem.**
	[ju lútɛm]

I, me	**unë, mua**
	[únə], [múa]
you (inform.)	**ti**
	[ti]
he	**ai**
	[ai]
she	**ajo**
	[ajó]
they (masc.)	**ata**
	[atá]
they (fem.)	**ato**
	[ató]
we	**ne**
	[nɛ]
you (pl)	**ju**
	[ju]
you (sg, form.)	**ju**
	[ju]

ENTRANCE	**HYRJE**
	[hýrjɛ]
EXIT	**DALJE**
	[dáljɛ]
OUT OF ORDER	**NUK FUNKSIONON**
	[nuk funksionón]
CLOSED	**MBYLLUR**
	[mbýɫuɼ]

OPEN | **HAPUR**
[hápur]

FOR WOMEN | **PËR FEMRA**
[pər fémra]

FOR MEN | **PËR MESHKUJ**
[pər méʃkuj]

Questions

Where?	**Ku?** [ku?]
Where to?	**Për ku?** [pər ku?]
Where from?	**Nga ku?** [ŋa ku?]
Why?	**Pse?** [psɛ?]
For what reason?	**Për çfarë arsye?** [pər tʃfárə arsýɛ?]
When?	**Kur?** [kur?]
How long?	**Sa kohë?** [sa kóhə?]
At what time?	**Në çfarë ore?** [nə tʃfárə órɛ?]
How much?	**Sa kushton?** [sa kuʃtón?]
Do you have ...?	**Keni ...?** [kéni ...?]
Where is ...?	**Ku ndodhet ...?** [ku ndóðɛt ...?]
What time is it?	**Sa është ora?** [sa ə́ʃtə óra?]
May I make a call?	**Mund të bëj një telefonatë?** [mund tə bəj ɲə tɛlɛfonátə?]
Who's there?	**Kush është?** [kuʃ ə́ʃtə?]
Can I smoke here?	**Mund të pi duhan këtu?** [mund tə pi duhán kətú?]
May I ...?	**Mund të ...?** [mund tə ...?]

Needs

I'd like ...	**Do të doja ...** [do tə dója ...]
I don't want ...	**Nuk dua ...** [nuk dúa ...]
I'm thirsty.	**Kam etje.** [kam étjɛ]
I want to sleep.	**Dua të fle.** [dúa tə flé]
I want ...	**Dua ...** [dúa ...]
to wash up	**të lahem** [tə láhɛm]
to brush my teeth	**të laj dhëmbët** [tə laj ðémbət]
to rest a while	**të pushoj pak** [tə puʃój pak]
to change my clothes	**të ndërrohem** [tə ndəróhɛm]
to go back to the hotel	**të kthehem në hotel** [tə kθéhɛm nə hotél]
to buy ...	**të blej ...** [tə blɛj ...]
to go to ...	**të shkoj në ...** [tə ʃkoj nə ...]
to visit ...	**të vizitoj ...** [tə vizitój ...]
to meet with ...	**të takohem me ...** [tə takóhɛm mɛ ...]
to make a call	**të bëj një telefonatë** [tə bəj ɲə tɛlɛfonátə]
I'm tired.	**Jam i /e/ lodhur.** [jam i /ɛ/ lóður]
We are tired.	**Jemi të lodhur.** [jémi tə lóður]
I'm cold.	**Kam ftohtë.** [kam ftóhtə]
I'm hot.	**Kam vapë.** [kam vápə]
I'm OK.	**Jam mirë.** [jam mírə]

I need to make a call.

Duhet të bëj një telefonatë.
[dúhɛt tə bəj ɲə tɛlɛfonátə]

I need to go to the restroom.

Duhet të shkoj në tualet.
[dúhɛt tə ʃkoj nə tualét]

I have to go.

Duhet të ik.
[dúhɛt tə ik]

I have to go now.

Duhet të ik tani.
[dúhɛt tə ik taní]

Asking for directions

Excuse me, ...
Më falni, ...
[mə fálni, ...]

Where is ...?
Ku ndodhet ...?
[ku ndóðɛt ...?]

Which way is ...?
Si shkohet në ...?
[si ʃkóhɛt nə ...?]

Could you help me, please?
Ju lutem, mund të më ndihmoni?
[ju lútɛm], [mund tə mə ndihmóni?]

I'm looking for ...
Kërkoj ...
[kərkój ...]

I'm looking for the exit.
Kërkoj daljen.
[kərkój dáljɛn]

I'm going to ...
Po shkoj në ...
[po ʃkoj nə ...]

Am I going the right way to ...?
A po shkoj siç duhet për në ...?
[a po ʃkoj sitʃ dúhɛt pər nə ...?]

Is it far?
Është larg?
[éʃtə larg?]

Can I get there on foot?
Mund të shkoj me këmbë deri atje?
[mund tə ʃkoj mɛ kémbə déri atjé?]

Can you show me on the map?
Mund të më tregoni në hartë?
[mund tə mə trɛgóni nə hártə?]

Show me where we are right now.
Më tregoni ku ndodhemi tani.
[mə trɛgóni ku ndóðɛmi taní]

Here
Këtu
[kətú]

There
Atje
[atjé]

This way
Këtej
[kətéj]

Turn right.
Kthehuni djathtas.
[kθéhuni djáθtas]

Turn left.
Kthehuni majtas.
[kθéhuni májtas]

first (second, third) turn
kthesa e parë (e dytë, e tretë)
[kθésa ɛ párə (ɛ dýtə), [ɛ trétə)]

to the right
djathtas
[djáθtas]

to the left

majtas
[májtas]

Go straight ahead.

ecni drejt
[étsni dréjt]

Signs

WELCOME!	**MIRË SE ERDHËT!** [mírə sɛ érðət!]
ENTRANCE	**HYRJE** [hýrjɛ]
EXIT	**DALJE** [dáljɛ]

PUSH	**SHTY** [ʃty]
PULL	**TËRHIQ** [tərhíc]
OPEN	**HAPUR** [hápuɾ]
CLOSED	**MBYLLUR** [mbýɫuɾ]

FOR WOMEN	**PËR FEMRA** [pər fémra]
FOR MEN	**PËR MESHKUJ** [pər méʃkuj]
GENTLEMEN, GENTS	**ZOTËRINJ** [zotəríɲ]
WOMEN	**ZONJA** [zóɲa]

DISCOUNTS	**ULJE** [úljɛ]
SALE	**ULJE** [úljɛ]
FREE	**FALAS** [fálas]
NEW!	**E RE!** [ɛ ré!]
ATTENTION!	**KUJDES!** [kujdés!]

NO VACANCIES	**NUK KA VENDE TË LIRA** [nuk ka véndɛ tə líra]
RESERVED	**REZERVUAR** [rɛzɛrvúaɾ]
ADMINISTRATION	**ADMINISTRATA** [administráta]
STAFF ONLY	**VETËM PËR PERSONELIN** [vétəm pər pɛrsonélin]

BEWARE OF THE DOG!	**KUJDES NGA QENI!** [kujdés ŋa céni!]
NO SMOKING!	**NDALOHET DUHANI!** [ndalóhɛt duháni!]
DO NOT TOUCH!	**MOS PREKNI!** [mos prékni!]
DANGEROUS	**I RREZIKSHËM** [i rɛzíkʃəm]
DANGER	**RREZIK** [rɛzík]
HIGH VOLTAGE	**VOLTAZH I LARTË** [voltáʒ i lártə]
NO SWIMMING!	**NDALOHET NOTI!** [ndalóhɛt nóti!]

OUT OF ORDER	**NUK FUNKSIONON** [nuk funksionón]
FLAMMABLE	**I DJEGSHËM** [i djégʃəm]
FORBIDDEN	**I NDALUAR** [i ndalúar]
NO TRESPASSING!	**NDALOHET KALIMI!** [ndalóhɛt kalími!]
WET PAINT	**BOJË E FRESKËT** [bójə ɛ fréskət]

CLOSED FOR RENOVATIONS	**MBYLLUR PËR RESTAURIM** [mbýɫur pər rɛstaurim]
WORKS AHEAD	**PO KRYHEN PUNIME** [po krýhɛn punímɛ]
DETOUR	**DEVIJIM** [dɛvijím]

Transportation. General phrases

plane	**avion** [avión]
train	**tren** [trɛn]
bus	**autobus** [autobús]
ferry	**traget** [tragét]
taxi	**taksi** [táksi]
car	**makinë** [makínə]
schedule	**orar** [orár]
Where can I see the schedule?	**Ku mund të shikoj oraret?** [ku mund tə ʃikój orárɛt?]
workdays (weekdays)	**ditë pune** [dítə púnɛ]
weekends	**fundjava** [fundjáva]
holidays	**pushime** [puʃímɛ]
DEPARTURE	**NISJE** [nísjɛ]
ARRIVAL	**MBËRRITJE** [mbərítjɛ]
DELAYED	**VONESË** [vonésə]
CANCELLED	**ANULUAR** [anulúar]
next (train, etc.)	**tjetër** [tjétər]
first	**parë** [párə]
last	**fundit** [fúndit]
When is the next ...?	**Kur është ... tjetër?** [kur éʃtə ... tjétər?]
When is the first ...?	**Kur është ... i parë?** [kur éʃtə ... i párə?]

When is the last ...?

Kur është ... i fundit?
[kur éʃtə ... i fúndit?]

transfer (change of trains, etc.)

ndërrim
[ndərím]

to make a transfer

të ndërroj
[tə ndərój]

Do I need to make a transfer?

Duhet të ndërroj?
[dúhɛt tə ndərój?]

Buying tickets

Where can I buy tickets?	**Ku mund të blej bileta?** [ku mund tə bléj biléta?]
ticket	**biletë** [bilétə]
to buy a ticket	**të blej biletë** [tə blɛj bilétə]
ticket price	**çmimi i biletës** [tʃmími i bilétəs]
Where to?	**Për ku?** [pər ku?]
To what station?	**Në cilin stacion?** [nə tsílin statsión?]
I need ...	**Më nevojitet ...** [mə nɛvojítɛt ...]
one ticket	**një biletë** [ɲə bilétə]
two tickets	**dy bileta** [dy biléta]
three tickets	**tre bileta** [trɛ biléta]
one-way	**vajtje** [vájtjɛ]
round-trip	**me kthim** [mɛ kθim]
first class	**klasi i parë** [klási i párə]
second class	**klasi i dytë** [klási i dýtə]
today	**sot** [sot]
tomorrow	**nesër** [nésər]
the day after tomorrow	**pasnesër** [pasnésər]
in the morning	**në mëngjes** [nə mənɟés]
in the afternoon	**në pasdite** [nə pasdítɛ]
in the evening	**në mbrëmje** [nə mbrə́mjɛ]

aisle seat

window seat

How much?

Can I pay by credit card?

ulëse në korridor
[úləsɛ nə koridór]

ulëse tek dritarja
[úləsɛ tɛk dritárja]

Sa kushton?
[sa kuʃtón?]

Mund të paguaj me kartelë krediti?
[mund tə pagúaj mɛ kartélə krɛdíti?]

Bus

bus	**autobus** [autobús]
intercity bus	**autobus urban** [autobús urbán]
bus stop	**stacion autobusi** [statsión autobúsi]
Where's the nearest bus stop?	**Ku ndodhet stacioni më i afërt i autobusit?** [ku ndóðɛt statsióni mə i áfərt i autobúsit?]
number (bus ~, etc.)	**numri** [númri]
Which bus do I take to get to …?	**Cilin autobus duhet të marr për të shkuar në …?** [tsílin autobús dúhɛt tə mar pər tə ʃkúar nə …?]
Does this bus go to …?	**A shkon ky autobus në …?** [a ʃkon ky autobús nə …?]
How frequent are the buses?	**Sa shpesh kalojnë autobusët?** [sa ʃpɛʃ kalójnə autobúsət?]
every 15 minutes	**çdo 15 minuta** [tʃdo pɛsəmbəðjétə minúta]
every half hour	**çdo gjysmë ore** [tʃdo ɟýsmə órɛ]
every hour	**çdo një orë** [tʃdo ɲə órə]
several times a day	**disa herë në ditë** [dísa hérə nə dítə]
… times a day	**… herë në ditë** [… hérə nə dítə]
schedule	**orari** [orári]
Where can I see the schedule?	**Ku mund të shikoj oraret?** [ku mund tə ʃikój orárɛt?]
When is the next bus?	**Kur është autobusi tjetër?** [kur ə́ʃtə autobúsi tjétər?]
When is the first bus?	**Kur është autobusi i parë?** [kur ə́ʃtə autobúsi i párə?]
When is the last bus?	**Kur është autobusi i fundit?** [kur ə́ʃtə autobúsi i fúndit?]

stop

stacion
[statsión]

next stop

stacioni tjetër
[statsióni tjétər]

last stop (terminus)

stacioni i fundit
[statsióni i fúndit]

Stop here, please.

Ju lutem, ndaloni këtu.
[ju lútɛm], [ndalóni kətú]

Excuse me, this is my stop.

Më falni, ky është stacioni im.
[mə fálni], [ky əʃtə statsióni im]

Train

train	**tren** [trɛn]
suburban train	**tren lokal** [trɛn lokál]
long-distance train	**tren** [trɛn]
train station	**stacion treni** [statsión trɛni]
Excuse me, where is the exit to the platform?	**Më falni, ku është dalja për në platformë?** [mə fálni], [ku ə́ʃtə dálja pər nə platfórmə?]

Does this train go to ...?	**A shkon ky tren në ...?** [a ʃkon ky trɛn nə ...?]
next train	**treni tjetër** [tréni tjétər]
When is the next train?	**Kur vjen treni tjetër?** [kur vjɛn tréni tjétər?]
Where can I see the schedule?	**Ku mund të shikoj oraret?** [ku mund tə ʃikój orárɛt?]
From which platform?	**Nga cila platformë?** [ŋa tsíla platfórmə?]
When does the train arrive in ...?	**Kur arrin treni në ...** [kur arín tréni nə ...]

Please help me.	**Ju lutem më ndihmoni.** [ju lútɛm mə ndihmóni]
I'm looking for my seat.	**Kërkoj ulësen time.** [kərkój úləsɛn tímɛ]
We're looking for our seats.	**Po kërkojmë ulëset tona.** [po kərkójmə úləsɛt tóna]
My seat is taken.	**ulësja ime është zënë.** [úləsja ímɛ ə́ʃtə zə́nə]
Our seats are taken.	**ulëset tona janë zënë.** [úləsɛt tóna jánə zə́nə]

I'm sorry but this is my seat.	**Më falni por kjo është ulësja ime.** [mə fálni por kjo ə́ʃtə úləsja ímɛ]
Is this seat taken?	**A është e zënë kjo ulëse?** [a ə́ʃtə ɛ zə́nə kjo úləsɛ?]
May I sit here?	**Mund të ulem këtu?** [mund tə úlɛm kətú?]

On the train. Dialogue (No ticket)

Ticket, please.

Biletën, ju lutem.
[bilétən], [ju lútɛm]

I don't have a ticket.

Nuk kam biletë.
[nuk kam bilétə]

I lost my ticket.

Humba biletën.
[húmba bilétən]

I forgot my ticket at home.

E harrova biletën në shtëpi.
[ɛ haróva bilétən nə ʃtəpí]

You can buy a ticket from me.

Mund të blini biletën tek unë.
[mund tə blíni bilétən tɛk únə]

You will also have to pay a fine.

Duhet gjithashtu të paguani gjobë.
[dúhɛt ɟiθaʃtú tə pagúani ɟóbə]

Okay.

Në rregull.
[nə réguɫ]

Where are you going?

Ku po shkoni?
[ku po ʃkóni?]

I'm going to ...

Po shkoj në ...
[po ʃkoj nə ...]

How much? I don't understand.

Sa kushton? Nuk kuptoj.
[sa kuʃtón? nuk kuptój]

Write it down, please.

Shkruajeni, ju lutem.
[ʃkrúajɛni], [ju lútɛm]

Okay. Can I pay with a credit card?

Në rregull. Mund të paguaj me kartelë krediti?
[nə réguɫ. mund tə pagúaj mɛ kartélə krɛdíti?]

Yes, you can.

Po, mundeni.
[po], [múndɛni]

Here's your receipt.

Urdhëroni faturën.
[urðəróni fatúrən]

Sorry about the fine.

Më vjen keq për gjobën.
[mə vjɛn kɛc pər ɟóbən]

That's okay. It was my fault.

S'ka gjë. ishte gabimi im.
[s'ka ɟə. íʃtɛ gabími im]

Enjoy your trip.

Rrugë të mbarë.
[rúgə tə mbárə]

Taxi

taxi	**taksi** [táksi]
taxi driver	**shofer taksie** [ʃofér taksíɛ]
to catch a taxi	**të kap taksi** [tə kap táksi]
taxi stand	**stacion për taksi** [statsión pər táksi]
Where can I get a taxi?	**Ku mund të gjej një taksi?** [ku mund tə ɟɛj ɲə táksi?]

to call a taxi	**thërras një taksi** [θərás ɲə táksi]
I need a taxi.	**Më nevojitet taksi.** [mə nɛvojítɛt táksi]
Right now.	**Tani.** [taní]
What is your address (location)?	**Cila është adresa juaj?** [tsíla éʃtə adrésa júaj?]
My address is ...	**Adresa ime është ...** [adrésa imɛ éʃtə ...]
Your destination?	**Destinacioni juaj?** [dɛstinatsióni júaj?]
Excuse me, ...	**Më falni, ...** [mə fálni, ...]
Are you available?	**Jeni i lirë?** [jéni i lírə?]
How much is it to get to ...?	**Sa kushton deri në ...?** [sa kuʃtón déri nə ...?]
Do you know where it is?	**E dini ku ndodhet?** [ɛ díni ku ndóðɛt?]

Airport, please.	**Në aeroport, ju lutem.** [nə aɛropórt], [ju lútɛm]
Stop here, please.	**Ju lutem, ndaloni këtu.** [ju lútɛm], [ndalóni kətú]
It's not here.	**Nuk është këtu.** [nuk éʃtə kətú]
This is the wrong address.	**Kjo është adresë e gabuar.** [kjo éʃtə adrésə ɛ gabúar]
Turn left.	**Kthehuni majtas.** [kθéhuni májtas]
Turn right.	**Kthehuni djathtas.** [kθéhuni djáθtas]

How much do I owe you?

Sa ju detyrohem?
[sa ju dɛtyróhɛm?]

I'd like a receipt, please.

Ju lutem, më jepni një faturë.
[ju lútɛm], [mə jépni ɲə fatúrə]

Keep the change.

Mbajeni kusurin.
[mbájɛni kusúrin]

Would you please wait for me?

Mund të më prisni, ju lutem?
[mund tə mə prísni], [ju lútɛm?]

five minutes

pesë minuta
[pésə minúta]

ten minutes

dhjetë minuta
[ðjétə minúta]

fifteen minutes

pesëmbëdhjetë minuta
[pɛsəmbəðjétə minúta]

twenty minutes

njëzet minuta
[ɲəzét minúta]

half an hour

gjysmë ore
[ɟýsmə órɛ]

Hotel

Hello.	**Përshëndetje.** [pərʃəndétjɛ]
My name is ...	**Më quajnë ...** [mə cúajnə ...]
I have a reservation.	**Kam një rezervim.** [kam ɲə rɛzɛrvím]
I need ...	**Më nevojitet ...** [mə nɛvojítɛt ...]
a single room	**dhomë teke** [ðómə tékɛ]
a double room	**dhomë dyshe** [ðómə dýʃɛ]
How much is that?	**Sa kushton?** [sa kuʃtón?]
That's a bit expensive.	**Është pak shtrenjtë.** [əʃtə pak ʃtréɲtə]
Do you have anything else?	**Keni ndonjë gjë tjetër?** [kéni ndóɲə ɟə tjétər?]
I'll take it.	**Do ta marr.** [do ta mar]
I'll pay in cash.	**Do paguaj me para në dorë.** [do pagúaj mɛ pará nə dórə]
I've got a problem.	**Kam një problem.** [kam ɲə problém]
My ... is broken.	**Më është prishur ...** [mə əʃtə príʃur ...]
My ... is out of order.	**Nuk funksionon ...** [nuk funksionón ...]
TV	**televizor** [tɛlɛvizór]
air conditioner	**kondicioner** [konditsionér]
tap	**çezma** [tʃézma]
shower	**dushi** [duʃí]
sink	**lavamani** [lavamáni]
safe	**kasaforta** [kasafórta]

door lock	**brava e derës** [bráva ɛ dérəs]
electrical outlet	**paneli elektrik** [panéli ɛlɛktrík]
hairdryer	**tharësja e flokëve** [θárəsja ɛ flókəvɛ]

I don't have ...	**Nuk kam ...** [nuk kam ...]
water	**ujë** [újə]
light	**drita** [dríta]
electricity	**korrent** [korént]

Can you give me ...?	**Mund të më jepni ...?** [mund tə mə jépni ...?]
a towel	**një peshqir** [ɲə pɛʃcír]
a blanket	**një çarçaf** [ɲə tʃartʃáf]
slippers	**shapka** [ʃápka]
a robe	**penuar** [pɛnuár]
shampoo	**shampo** [ʃampó]
soap	**sapun** [sapún]

I'd like to change rooms.	**Dua të ndryshoj dhomën.** [dúa tə ndryʃój ðómən]
I can't find my key.	**Nuk po gjej çelësin.** [nuk po ɟɛj tʃéləsin]
Could you open my room, please?	**Mund të më hapni derën, ju lutem?** [mund tə mə hápni dérən], [ju lútɛm?]
Who's there?	**Kush është?** [kuʃ éʃtə?]
Come in!	**Hyni!** [hýni!]
Just a minute!	**Një minutë!** [ɲə minútə!]
Not right now, please.	**Jo tani, ju lutem.** [jo taní], [ju lútɛm]

Come to my room, please.	**Ju lutem, ejani në dhomë.** [ju lútɛm], [éjani nə ðómə]
I'd like to order food service.	**Dua të porosisja ushqim.** [dúa tə porosísja uʃcím]
My room number is ...	**Numri i dhomës është ...** [númri i ðóməs éʃtə ...]

I'm leaving ...

Po largohem ...
[po largóhɛm ...]

We're leaving ...

Po largohemi ...
[po largóhɛmi ...]

right now

tani
[taní]

this afternoon

këtë pasdite
[kə́tə pasdítɛ]

tonight

sonte
[sóntɛ]

tomorrow

nesër
[nésər]

tomorrow morning

nesër në mëngjes
[nésər nə məɲɟés]

tomorrow evening

nesër në mbrëmje
[nésər nə mbrə́mjɛ]

the day after tomorrow

pasnesër
[pasnésər]

I'd like to pay.

Dua të paguaj.
[dúa tə pagúaj]

Everything was wonderful.

Gjithçka ishte e mrekullueshme.
[ɟiθʧká íʃtɛ ɛ mrɛkuɫúɛʃmɛ]

Where can I get a taxi?

Ku mund të gjej një taksi?
[ku mund tə ɟɛj ɲə táksi?]

Would you call a taxi for me, please?

Mund të më thërrisni një taksi, ju lutem?
[mund tə mə θərrísni ɲə táksi], [ju lútɛm?]

Restaurant

Can I look at the menu, please?	**Mund të shoh menynë, ju lutem?** [mund tə ʃoh mɛnýnə], [ju lútɛm?]
Table for one.	**Tavolinë për një person.** [tavolínə pər ɲə pɛrsón]
There are two (three, four) of us.	**Jemi dy (tre, katër) vetë.** [jémi dy (trɛ], [kátər) vétə]
Smoking	**Lejohet duhani** [lɛjóhɛt duháni]
No smoking	**Ndalohet duhani** [ndalóhɛt duháni]
Excuse me! (addressing a waiter)	**Më falni!** [mə fálni!]
menu	**menyja** [mɛnýja]
wine list	**menyja e verave** [mɛnýja ɛ véravɛ]
The menu, please.	**Menynë, ju lutem.** [mɛnýnə], [ju lútɛm]
Are you ready to order?	**Jeni gati për të dhënë porosinë?** [jéni gáti pər tə ðénə porosínə?]
What will you have?	**Çfarë do të merrni?** [tʃfárə do tə mérni?]
I'll have ...	**Do të marr ...** [do tə mar ...]
I'm a vegetarian.	**Jam vegjetarian /vegjetariane/.** [jam vɛɟɛtarián /vɛɟɛtariánɛ/]
meat	**mish** [miʃ]
fish	**peshk** [pɛʃk]
vegetables	**perime** [pɛrímɛ]
Do you have vegetarian dishes?	**Keni gatime për vegjetarianë?** [kéni gatímɛ pər vɛɟɛtariánə?]
I don't eat pork.	**Nuk ha mish derri.** [nuk ha miʃ déri]
Band-Aid	**Ai /Ajo/ nuk ha mish.** [aí /ajó/ nuk ha miʃ]
I am allergic to ...	**Kam alergji nga ...** [kam alɛɾɟí ŋa ...]

Would you please bring me ...	**Mund të më sillni ...** [mund tə mə síɬni ...]
salt | pepper | sugar	**kripë | piper | sheqer** [krípə | pipér | ʃɛcér]
coffee | tea | dessert	**kafe | çaj | ëmbëlsirë** [káfɛ | tʃaj | əmbəlsírə]
water | sparkling | plain	**ujë | me gaz | pa gaz** [újə | mɛ gaz | pa gaz]
a spoon | fork | knife	**një lugë | pirun | thikë** [ɲə lúgə | pirún | θíkə]
a plate | napkin	**një pjatë | pecetë** [ɲə pjátə | pɛtsétə]

Enjoy your meal!	**Ju bëftë mirë!** [ju béftə mírə!]
One more, please.	**Dhe një tjetër, ju lutem.** [ðɛ ɲə tjétər], [ju lútɛm]
It was very delicious.	**ishte shumë e shijshme.** [iʃtɛ ʃúmə ɛ ʃíjʃmɛ]

check | change | tip	**llogari | kusur | bakshish** [ɬogarí | kusúr | bakʃíʃ]
Check, please. (Could I have the check, please?)	**Llogarinë, ju lutem.** [ɬogarínə], [ju lútɛm]
Can I pay by credit card?	**Mund të paguaj me kartelë krediti?** [mund tə pagúaj mɛ kartélə krɛdíti?]
I'm sorry, there's a mistake here.	**Më falni por ka një gabim këtu.** [mə fálni por ka ɲə gabím kətú]

Shopping

Can I help you?	Mund t'ju ndihmoj? [mund t'ju ndihmój?]
Do you have ...?	Keni ...? [kéni ...?]
I'm looking for ...	Kërkoj ... [kərkój ...]
I need ...	Më nevojitet ... [mə nɛvojítɛt ...]

I'm just looking.	Thjesht po shoh. [θjɛʃt po ʃoh]
We're just looking.	Thjesht po shohim. [θjɛʃt po ʃóhim]
I'll come back later.	Do vij më vonë. [do vij mə vónə]
We'll come back later.	Do vijmë më vonë. [do víjmə mə vónə]
discounts	sale	ulje çmimesh	ulje [úljɛ tʃmímɛʃ	úljɛ]

Would you please show me ...	Ju lutem mund të më tregoni ... [ju lútɛm mund tə mə trɛgóni ...]
Would you please give me ...	Ju lutem mund të më jepni ... [ju lútɛm mund tə mə jépni ...]
Can I try it on?	Mund ta provoj? [mund ta provój?]
Excuse me, where's the fitting room?	Më falni, ku është dhoma e provës? [mə fálni], [ku ə́ʃtə ðóma ɛ próvəs?]
Which color would you like?	Çfarë ngjyre e doni? [tʃfárə ɲɟýrɛ ɛ dóni?]
size	length	numri	gjatësia [númri	ɟatəsía]
How does it fit?	Si ju rri? [si ju ri?]

How much is it?	Sa kushton? [sa kuʃtón?]
That's too expensive.	Është shumë shtrenjtë. [ə́ʃtə ʃúmə ʃtréɲtə]
I'll take it.	Do ta marr. [do ta mar]
Excuse me, where do I pay?	Më falni, ku duhet të paguaj? [mə fálni], [ku dúhɛt tə pagúaj?]

Will you pay in cash or credit card?

Do paguani me para në dorë apo kartelë krediti?
[do pagúani mɛ pará nə dórə apo kartélə krɛdíti?]

In cash | with credit card

Me para në dorë | me kartelë krediti
[mɛ pará nə dórə | mɛ kartélə krɛdíti]

Do you want the receipt?

Dëshironi faturën?
[dəʃiróni fatúrən?]

Yes, please.

Po faleminderit.
[po falɛmindérit]

No, it's OK.

Jo, s'ka problem.
[jo], [s'ka problém]

Thank you. Have a nice day!

Faleminderit. Ditë të mbarë!
[falɛmindérit. dítə tə mbárə!]

In town

Excuse me, ...
Më falni, ju lutem.
[mə fálni], [ju lútɛm]

I'm looking for ...
Kërkoj ...
[kərkój ...]

the subway
metronë
[mɛtrónə]

my hotel
hotelin
[hotélin]

the movie theater
kinemanë
[kinɛmánə]

a taxi stand
një stacion për taksi
[ɲə statsión pər táksi]

an ATM
një bankomat
[ɲə bankomát]

a foreign exchange office
një zyrë shkëmbimi parash
[ɲə zýrə ʃkəmbími paráʃ]

an internet café
një internet kafe
[ɲə intɛrnét káfɛ]

... street
rrugën ...
[rúgən ...]

this place
këtë vend
[kə́tə vɛnd]

Do you know where ... is?
Dini ku ndodhet ...?
[díni ku ndóðɛt ...?]

Which street is this?
Cila rrugë është kjo?
[tsíla rúgə ə́ʃtə kjó?]

Show me where we are right now.
Më tregoni ku ndodhemi tani.
[mə trɛgóni ku ndóðɛmi taní]

Can I get there on foot?
Mund të shkoj me këmbë deri atje?
[mund tə ʃkoj mɛ kə́mbə dɛ́ri atjé?]

Do you have a map of the city?
Keni hartë të qytetit?
[kéni hártə tə cytétit?]

How much is a ticket to get in?
Sa kushton një biletë hyrje?
[sa kuʃtón ɲə bilétə hýrjɛ?]

Can I take pictures here?
Mund të bëj fotografi këtu?
[mund tə bəj fotografí kətú?]

Are you open?
Jeni të hapur?
[jéni tə hápur?]

When do you open?

Kur hapeni?
[kur hápɛni?]

When do you close?

Kur mbylleni?
[kur mbýɫɛni?]

Money

money	**para** [pará]
cash	**para në dorë** [pará nə dórə]
paper money	**kartëmonedha** [kartəmonéða]
loose change	**kusur** [kusúr]
check | change | tip	**llogari | kusur | bakshish** [ɫogarí | kusúr | bakʃíʃ]

credit card	**kartelë krediti** [kartélə krɛdíti]
wallet	**portofol** [portofól]
to buy	**të blej** [tə blɛj]
to pay	**të paguaj** [tə pagúaj]
fine	**gjobë** [ɟóbə]
free	**falas** [fálas]

Where can I buy ...?	**Ku mund të blej ...?** [ku mund tə blɛj ...?]
Is the bank open now?	**Është banka e hapur tani?** [əʃtə bánka ɛ hápur taní?]
When does it open?	**Kur hapet?** [kur hápɛt?]
When does it close?	**Kur mbyllet?** [kur mbýɫɛt?]

How much?	**Sa kushton?** [sa kuʃtón?]
How much is this?	**Sa kushton kjo?** [sa kuʃtón kjo?]
That's too expensive.	**Është shumë shtrenjtë.** [əʃtə ʃúmə ʃtréɲtə]

Excuse me, where do I pay?	**Më falni, ku duhet të paguaj?** [mə fálni], [ku dúhɛt tə pagúaj?]
Check, please.	**Llogarinë, ju lutem.** [ɫogarínə], [ju lútɛm]

Can I pay by credit card?

Mund të paguaj me kartelë krediti?
[mund tə pagúaj mɛ kartélə krɛdíti?]

Is there an ATM here?

Ka ndonjë bankomat këtu?
[ka ndóɲə bankomát kətú?]

I'm looking for an ATM.

Kërkoj një bankomat.
[kərkój ɲə bankomát]

I'm looking for a foreign exchange office.

Kërkoj një zyrë të këmbimit valutor.
[kərkój ɲə zýrə tə kəmbímit valutór]

I'd like to change ...

Dua të këmbej ...
[dúa tə kəmbéj ...]

What is the exchange rate?

Sa është kursi i këmbimit?
[sa ə́ʃtə kúrsi i kəmbímit?]

Do you need my passport?

Ju duhet pasaporta ime?
[ju dúhɛt pasapórta ímɛ?]

Time

What time is it?	**Sa është ora?** [sa ə́ʃtə óra?]
When?	**Kur?** [kur?]
At what time?	**Në çfarë ore?** [nə tʃfárə órɛ?]
now | later | after …	**tani | më vonë | pas …** [taní | mə vónə | pas …]
one o'clock	**ora një** [óra ɲə]
one fifteen	**një e çerek** [ɲə ɛ tʃɛrék]
one thirty	**një e tridhjetë** [ɲə ɛ triðjétə]
one forty-five	**një e dyzet e pesë** [ɲə ɛ dyzét ɛ pésə]
one | two | three	**një | dy | tre** [ɲə | dy | trɛ]
four | five | six	**katër | pesë | gjashtë** [kátər | pésə | ɟáʃtə]
seven | eight | nine	**shtatë | tetë | nëntë** [ʃtátə | tétə | néntə]
ten | eleven | twelve	**dhjetë | njëmbëdhjetë | dymbëdhjetë** [ðjétə | ɲəmbəðjétə | dymbəðjétə]
in …	**për …** [pər …]
five minutes	**pesë minuta** [pésə minúta]
ten minutes	**dhjetë minuta** [ðjétə minúta]
fifteen minutes	**pesëmbëdhjetë minuta** [pɛsəmbəðjétə minúta]
twenty minutes	**njëzet minuta** [ɲəzét minúta]
half an hour	**gjysmë ore** [ɟýsmə órɛ]
an hour	**një orë** [ɲə órə]

in the morning	**në mëngjes** [nə mənɟés]
early in the morning	**në mëngjes herët** [nə mənɟés hérət]
this morning	**sot në mëngjes** [sot nə mənɟés]
tomorrow morning	**nesër në mëngjes** [nésər nə mənɟés]
in the middle of the day	**në mesditë** [nə mɛsdítə]
in the afternoon	**në pasdite** [nə pasdítɛ]
in the evening	**në mbrëmje** [nə mbrémjɛ]
tonight	**sonte** [sóntɛ]
at night	**natën** [nátən]
yesterday	**dje** [djé]
today	**sot** [sot]
tomorrow	**nesër** [nésər]
the day after tomorrow	**pasnesër** [pasnésər]
What day is it today?	**Çfarë dite është sot?** [tʃfárə dítɛ éʃtə sot?]
It's ...	**Është ...** [éʃtə ...]
Monday	**E hënë** [ɛ hénə]
Tuesday	**E martë** [ɛ mártə]
Wednesday	**E mërkurë** [ɛ mərkúrə]
Thursday	**E enjte** [ɛ éɲtɛ]
Friday	**E premte** [ɛ prémtɛ]
Saturday	**E shtunë** [ɛ ʃtúnə]
Sunday	**E diel** [ɛ díɛl]

Greetings. Introductions

Hello.
Përshëndetje.
[pərʃəndétjɛ]

Pleased to meet you.
Kënaqësi që u njohëm.
[kənacəsí cə u ɲóhəm]

Me too.
Gjithashtu.
[ɟiθaʃtú]

I'd like you to meet ...
Ju prezantoj me ...
[ju prɛzantój mɛ ...]

Nice to meet you.
Gëzohem që u njohëm.
[gəzóhɛm cə u ɲóhəm]

How are you?
Si jeni?
[si jéni?]

My name is ...
Më quajnë ...
[mə cúajnə ...]

His name is ...
Ai quhet ...
[ai cúhɛt ...]

Her name is ...
Ajo quhet ...
[ajó cúhɛt ...]

What's your name?
Si quheni?
[si cúhɛni?]

What's his name?
Si e quajnë?
[si ɛ cúajnə?]

What's her name?
Si e quajnë?
[si ɛ cúajnə?]

What's your last name?
Si e keni mbiemrin?
[si ɛ kéni mbiémrin?]

You can call me ...
Mund të më thërrisni ...
[mund tə mə θərísni ...]

Where are you from?
Nga jeni?
[ŋa jéni?]

I'm from ...
Jam nga ...
[jam ŋa ...]

What do you do for a living?
Me çfarë merreni?
[mɛ tʃfárə mérɛni?]

Who is this?
Kush është ky?
[kuʃ əʃtə ky?]

Who is he?
Kush është ai?
[kuʃ əʃtə ái?]

Who is she?	**Kush është ajo?** [kuʃ əʃtə ajó?]
Who are they?	**Kush janë ata?** [kuʃ jánə atá?]

This is ...	**Ky /Kjo/ është ...** [ky /kjo/ əʃtə ...]
my friend (masc.)	**shoku im** [ʃóku im]
my friend (fem.)	**shoqja ime** [ʃócja ímɛ]
my husband	**bashkëshorti im** [baʃkəʃórti im]
my wife	**bashkëshortja ime** [baʃkəʃórtja imɛ]

my father	**babai im** [babái im]
my mother	**nëna ime** [nɛ́na ímɛ]
my brother	**vëllai im** [vəɬái im]
my sister	**motra ime** [mótra ímɛ]
my son	**djali im** [djáli im]
my daughter	**vajza ime** [vájza ímɛ]

This is our son.	**Ky është djali ynë.** [ky əʃtə djáli ýnə]
This is our daughter.	**Kjo është vajza jonë.** [kjo əʃtə vájza jónə]
These are my children.	**Këta janë fëmijët e mi.** [kətá jánə fəmíjət ɛ mi]
These are our children.	**Këta janë fëmijët tanë.** [kətá jánə fəmíjət tánə]

Farewells

Good bye!	**Mirupafshim!** [mirupáfʃim!]
Bye! (inform.)	**Pafshim!** [páfʃim!]
See you tomorrow.	**Shihemi nesër.** [ʃíhɛmi nésər]
See you soon.	**Shihemi së shpejti.** [ʃíhɛmi sə ʃpéjti]
See you at seven.	**Shihemi në orën shtatë.** [ʃíhɛmi nə órən ʃtátə]
Have fun!	**ia kalofshi mirë!** [ía kalófʃi mírə!]
Talk to you later.	**Flasim më vonë.** [flásim mə vónə]
Have a nice weekend.	**Fundjavë të këndshme.** [fundjávə tə kəndʃmɛ]
Good night.	**Natën e mirë.** [nátən ɛ mírə]
It's time for me to go.	**erdhi koha të ik.** [érði kóha tə ik]
I have to go.	**Duhet të ik.** [dúhɛt tə ik]
I will be right back.	**Kthehem menjëherë.** [kθéhɛm mɛɲəhérə]
It's late.	**Është vonë.** [ə́ʃtə vónə]
I have to get up early.	**Duhet të ngrihem herët.** [dúhɛt tə ŋríhɛm hérət]
I'm leaving tomorrow.	**Do ik nesër.** [do ik nésər]
We're leaving tomorrow.	**Do ikim nesër.** [do íkim nésər]
Have a nice trip!	**Udhëtim të mbarë!** [uðətím tə mbárə!]
It was nice meeting you.	**ishte kënaqësi.** [íʃtɛ kənacəsí]
It was nice talking to you.	**ishte kënaqësi që folëm.** [íʃtɛ kənacəsí cə fóləm]
Thanks for everything.	**Faleminderit për gjithçka.** [falɛmindérit pər ɟíθtʃka]

I had a very good time.

ia kalova shumë mirë.
[ía kalóva ʃúmə mírə]

We had a very good time.

ia kaluam shumë mirë.
[ía kalúam ʃúmə mírə]

It was really great.

ishte vërtet fantastike.
[íʃtɛ vərtét fantastíkɛ]

I'm going to miss you.

Do më marrë malli.
[do mə márə máłi]

We're going to miss you.

Do na marrë malli.
[do na márə máłi]

Good luck!

Suksese!
[suksésɛ!]

Say hi to ...

I bën të fala ...
[i bən tə fála ...]

Foreign language

I don't understand.	**Nuk kuptoj.** [nuk kuptój]
Write it down, please.	**Shkruajeni, ju lutem.** [ʃkrúajɛni], [ju lútɛm]
Do you speak ...?	**Flisni ...?** [flísni ...?]

I speak a little bit of ...	**Flas pak ...** [flás pak ...]
English	**Anglisht** [aŋlíʃt]
Turkish	**Turqisht** [turcíʃt]
Arabic	**Arabisht** [arabíʃt]
French	**Frëngjisht** [frənɟíʃt]

German	**Gjermanisht** [ɟɛrmaníʃt]
Italian	**Italisht** [italíʃt]
Spanish	**Spanjisht** [spaɲíʃt]
Portuguese	**Portugalisht** [portugalíʃt]
Chinese	**Kinezisht** [kinɛzíʃt]
Japanese	**Japonisht** [japoníʃt]

Can you repeat that, please.	**Mund ta përsërisni, ju lutem.** [mund ta pərsərísni], [ju lútɛm]
I understand.	**Kuptoj.** [kuptój]
I don't understand.	**Nuk kuptoj.** [nuk kuptój]
Please speak more slowly.	**Ju lutem, flisni më ngadalë.** [ju lútɛm], [flísni mə ŋadálə]

Is that correct? (Am I saying it right?)	**E saktë?** [ɛ sáktə?]
What is this? (What does this mean?)	**Çfarë është kjo?** [tʃfárə éʃtə kjó?]

Apologies

Excuse me, please.	**Më falni.** [mə fálni]
I'm sorry.	**Më vjen keq.** [mə vjɛn kɛc]
I'm really sorry.	**Më vjen shumë keq.** [mə vjɛn ʃúmə kɛc]
Sorry, it's my fault.	**Më fal, është faji im.** [mə fal], [ə́ʃtə fáji im]
My mistake.	**Gabimi im.** [gabími im]

May I ...?	**Mund të ...?** [mund tə ...?]
Do you mind if I ...?	**Ju vjen keq nëse ...?** [ju vjɛn kɛc nə́sɛ ...?]
It's OK.	**Është në rregull.** [ə́ʃtə nə réguɫ]
It's all right.	**Është në rregull.** [ə́ʃtə nə réguɫ]
Don't worry about it.	**Mos u shqetësoni.** [mos u ʃcɛtəsóni]

Agreement

Yes.	**Po.** [po]
Yes, sure.	**Po, sigurisht.** [po], [siguríʃt]
OK (Good!)	**Në rregull.** [nə réguɫ]
Very well.	**Shumë mirë.** [ʃúmə mírə]
Certainly!	**Sigurisht!** [siguríʃt!]
I agree.	**Jam dakord.** [jam dakórd]
That's correct.	**E saktë.** [ɛ sáktə]
That's right.	**E drejtë.** [ɛ dréjtə]
You're right.	**Keni të drejtë.** [kéni tə dréjtə]
I don't mind.	**S'e kam problem.** [s'ɛ kam problém]
Absolutely right.	**Absolutisht e drejtë.** [absolutíʃt ɛ dréjtə]
It's possible.	**Është e mundur.** [ə́ʃtə ɛ múndur]
That's a good idea.	**Ide e mirë.** [idé ɛ mírə]
I can't say no.	**Nuk them dot jo.** [nuk θɛm dot jo]
I'd be happy to.	**Është kënaqësi.** [ə́ʃtə kənacəsí]
With pleasure.	**Me kënaqësi.** [mɛ kənacəsí]

Refusal. Expressing doubt

No.

Jo.
[jo]

Certainly not.

Sigurisht që jo.
[siguríʃt cə jo]

I don't agree.

Nuk jam dakord.
[nuk jam dakórd]

I don't think so.

Nuk ma ha mendja.
[nuk ma ha méndja]

It's not true.

Nuk është e vërtetë.
[nuk əʃtə ε vərtétə]

You are wrong.

E keni gabim.
[ε kéni gabím]

I think you are wrong.

Më duket se e keni gabim.
[mə dúkεt sε ε kéni gabím]

I'm not sure.

Nuk jam i sigurt.
[nuk jam i sígurt]

It's impossible.

Është e pamundur.
[əʃtə ε pámundur]

Nothing of the kind (sort)!

Asgjë e këtij lloji!
[asɟə ε kətíj ɫóji!]

The exact opposite.

Krejt e kundërta.
[kréjt ε kúndərta]

I'm against it.

Jam kundër.
[jam kúndər]

I don't care.

Nuk më intereson.
[nuk mə intεrεsón]

I have no idea.

Nuk e kam idenë.
[nuk ε kam idénə]

I doubt it.

Dyshoj.
[dyʃój]

Sorry, I can't.

Më falni, nuk mundem.
[mə fálni], [nuk múndεm]

Sorry, I don't want to.

Më vjen keq, nuk dua.
[mə vjεn kεc], [nuk dúa]

Thank you, but I don't need this.

**Faleminderit, por s'kam nevojë
për këtë.**
[falεmindérit], [por s'kam nεvójə
pər kətə]

It's getting late.

Po shkon vonë.
[po ʃkon vónə]

I have to get up early.

Duhet të ngrihem herët.
[dúhɛt tə ŋɾíhɛm hérət]

I don't feel well.

Nuk ndihem mirë.
[nuk ndíhɛm mírə]

Expressing gratitude

Thank you.
Faleminderit.
[falɛmindérit]

Thank you very much.
Faleminderit shumë.
[falɛmindérit ʃúmə]

I really appreciate it.
E vlerësoj shumë.
[ɛ vlɛrəsój ʃúmə]

I'm really grateful to you.
Ju jam shumë mirënjohës.
[ju jam ʃúmə mirəɲóhəs]

We are really grateful to you.
Ju jemi shumë mirënjohës.
[ju jémi ʃúmə mirəɲóhəs]

Thank you for your time.
Faleminderit për kohën që më kushtuat.
[falɛmindérit pər kóhən cə mə kuʃtúat]

Thanks for everything.
Faleminderit për gjithçka.
[falɛmindérit pər ɟíθtʃka]

Thank you for …
Faleminderit për …
[falɛmindérit pər …]

your help
ndihmën tuaj
[ndíhmən túaj]

a nice time
kohën e këndshme
[kóhən ɛ kéndʃmɛ]

a wonderful meal
një vakt i mrekullueshëm
[ɲə vakt i mrɛkuɫúɛʃəm]

a pleasant evening
një mbrëmje e këndshme
[ɲə mbrémjɛ ɛ kéndʃmɛ]

a wonderful day
një ditë e mrekullueshme
[ɲə dítə ɛ mrɛkuɫúɛʃmɛ]

an amazing journey
një udhëtim i mahnitshëm
[ɲə uðətím i mahnítʃəm]

Don't mention it.
Mos u shqetësoni fare.
[mos u ʃcɛtəsóni fárɛ]

You are welcome.
Ju lutem.
[ju lútɛm]

Any time.
Në çdo kohë.
[nə tʃdo kóhə]

My pleasure.
Kënaqësia ime.
[kənacəsía ímɛ]

Forget it.

Harroje.
[harójɛ]

Don't worry about it.

Mos u shqetësoni.
[mos u ʃcɛtəsóni]

Congratulations. Best wishes

Congratulations! **Urime!**
[urímɛ!]

Happy birthday! **Gëzuar ditëlindjen!**
[gəzúar ditəlíndjɛn!]

Merry Christmas! **Gëzuar Krishtlindjet!**
[gəzúar kriʃtlíndjɛt!]

Happy New Year! **Gëzuar Vitin e Ri!**
[gəzúar vítin ɛ ɾi!]

Happy Easter! **Gëzuar Pashkët!**
[gəzúar páʃkət!]

Happy Hanukkah! **Gëzuar Hanukkah!**
[gəzúar hanúkkah!]

I'd like to propose a toast. **Dua të ngre një dolli.**
[dúa tə ŋɾé ɲə doɫí]

Cheers! **Gëzuar!**
[gəzúar!]

Let's drink to …! **Le të pijmë në shëndetin e …!**
[lɛ tə píjmə nə ʃəndétin ɛ …!]

To our success! **Për suksesin tonë!**
[pər suksésin tónə!]

To your success! **Për suksesin tuaj!**
[pər suksésin túaj!]

Good luck! **Suksese!**
[suksésɛ!]

Have a nice day! **Uroj një ditë të mbarë!**
[urój ɲə dítə tə mbárə!]

Have a good holiday! **Uroj pushime të këndshme!**
[urój puʃímɛ tə kəndʃmɛ!]

Have a safe journey! **Udhëtim të mbarë!**
[uðətím tə mbárə!]

I hope you get better soon! **Ju dëshiroj shërim të shpejtë!**
[ju dəʃirój ʃərím tə ʃpéjtə!]

Socializing

Why are you sad?	**Pse jeni i /e/ mërzitur?** [psɛ jéni i /ɛ/ mərzítur?]
Smile! Cheer up!	**Buzëqeshni! Gëzohuni!** [buzəcéʃni! gəzóhuni!]
Are you free tonight?	**Je i /e/ lirë sonte?** [jɛ i /ɛ/ lírə sóntɛ?]
May I offer you a drink?	**Mund t'ju ofroj një pije?** [mund t'ju ofrój ɲə píjɛ?]
Would you like to dance?	**Doni të kërcejmë?** [dóni tə kərtséjmə?]
Let's go to the movies.	**Shkojmë në kinema.** [ʃkójmə nə kinɛmá]
May I invite you to ...?	**Mund t'ju ftoj ...?** [mund t'ju ftoj ...?]
a restaurant	**në restorant** [nə rɛstoránt]
the movies	**në kinema** [nə kinɛmá]
the theater	**në teatër** [nə tɛátər]
go for a walk	**për një shëtitje** [pər ɲə ʃətítjɛ]
At what time?	**Në çfarë ore?** [nə tʃfárə órɛ?]
tonight	**sonte** [sóntɛ]
at six	**në gjashtë** [nə ɟáʃtə]
at seven	**në shtatë** [nə ʃtátə]
at eight	**në tetë** [nə tétə]
at nine	**në nëntë** [nə néntə]
Do you like it here?	**Ju pëlqen këtu?** [ju pəlcén kətú?]
Are you here with someone?	**Keni ardhur të shoqëruar?** [kéni árður tə ʃocərúar?]
I'm with my friend.	**Jam me një shok /shoqe/.** [jam mɛ ɲə ʃok /ʃócɛ/]

I'm with my friends.	**Jam me shoqëri.** [jam mɛ ʃocərí]
No, I'm alone.	**Jo, jam vetëm.** [jo], [jam vétəm]

Do you have a boyfriend?	**Ke të dashur?** [kɛ tə dáʃur?]
I have a boyfriend.	**Kam të dashur.** [kam tə dáʃur]
Do you have a girlfriend?	**Ke të dashur?** [kɛ tə dáʃur?]
I have a girlfriend.	**Kam të dashur.** [kam tə dáʃur]

Can I see you again?	**Mund të takohemi përsëri?** [mund tə takóhɛmi pərsərí?]
Can I call you?	**Mund të të telefonoj?** [mund tə tə tɛlɛfonój?]
Call me. (Give me a call.)	**Më telefono.** [mə tɛlɛfonó]
What's your number?	**Cili është numri yt?** [tsíli əʃtə númri yt?]
I miss you.	**Më mungon.** [mə muŋón]

You have a beautiful name.	**Keni emër të bukur.** [kéni émər tə búkur]
I love you.	**Të dua.** [tə dúa]
Will you marry me?	**Do martohesh me mua?** [do martóheʃ mɛ múa?]
You're kidding!	**Bëni shaka!** [béni ʃaká!]
I'm just kidding.	**Bëj shaka.** [bəj ʃaká]

Are you serious?	**E keni seriozisht?** [ɛ kéni sɛriozíʃt?]
I'm serious.	**E kam seriozisht.** [ɛ kam sɛriozíʃt]
Really?!	**Vërtet?!** [vərtét?!]
It's unbelievable!	**E pabesueshme!** [ɛ pabɛsúɛʃmɛ!]
I don't believe you.	**S'ju besoj.** [s'ju bɛsój]
I can't.	**S'mundem.** [s'múndɛm]
I don't know.	**Nuk e di.** [nuk ɛ di]
I don't understand you.	**Nuk ju kuptoj.** [nuk ju kuptój]

Please go away.

Leave me alone!

Ju lutem largohuni.
[ju lútɛm largóhuni]

Më lini të qetë!
[mə líni tə cétə!]

I can't stand him.

You are disgusting!

I'll call the police!

Se duroj dot.
[sɛ durój dot]

Jeni të neveritshëm!
[jéni tə nɛvɛrítʃəm!]

Do thërras policinë!
[do θərás politsínə!]

Sharing impressions. Emotions

I like it.	**Më pëlqen.**
	[mə pəlcén]
Very nice.	**Shumë bukur**
	[ʃúmə búkur]
That's great!	**Fantastike!**
	[fantastíkɛ!]
It's not bad.	**Nuk është keq.**
	[nuk əʃtə kɛc]

I don't like it.	**Nuk më pëlqen.**
	[nuk mə pəlcén]
It's not good.	**Nuk është mirë.**
	[nuk əʃtə mírə]
It's bad.	**Është keq.**
	[əʃtə kɛc]
It's very bad.	**Është shumë keq.**
	[əʃtə ʃúmə kɛc]
It's disgusting.	**Është e shpifur.**
	[əʃtə ɛ ʃpífur]

I'm happy.	**Jam i /e/ lumtur.**
	[jam i /ɛ/ lúmtur]
I'm content.	**Jam i /e/ kënaqur.**
	[jam i /ɛ/ kənácur]
I'm in love.	**Jam i /e/ dashuruar.**
	[jam i /ɛ/ daʃurúar]
I'm calm.	**Jam i /e/ qetë.**
	[jam i /ɛ/ cétə]
I'm bored.	**Jam i /e/ mërzitur.**
	[jam i /ɛ/ mərzítur]

I'm tired.	**Jam i /e/ lodhur.**
	[jam i /ɛ/ lóður]
I'm sad.	**Jam i /e/ trishtuar.**
	[jam i /ɛ/ triʃtúar]

I'm frightened.	**Jam i /e/ frikësuar.**
	[jam i /ɛ/ frikəsúar]
I'm angry.	**Jam i /e/ zemëruar.**
	[jam i /ɛ/ zɛmərúar]
I'm worried.	**Jam i /e/ shqetësuar.**
	[jam i /ɛ/ ʃcɛtəsúar]
I'm nervous.	**Jam nervoz /nervoze/.**
	[jam nɛrvóz /nɛrvózɛ/]

I'm jealous. (envious)

Jam xheloz /xheloze/.
[jam dʒɛlóz /dʒɛlózɛ/]

I'm surprised.

Jam i /e/ befasuar.
[jam i /ɛ/ bɛfasúar]

I'm perplexed.

Jam i /e/ hutuar.
[jam i /ɛ/ hutúar]

Problems. Accidents

I've got a problem.	**Kam një problem.** [kam ɲə problém]
We've got a problem.	**Kemi një problem.** [kémi ɲə problém]
I'm lost.	**Kam humbur.** [kam húmbuɾ]
I missed the last bus (train).	**Humba autobusin e fundit.** [húmba autobúsin ɛ fúndit]
I don't have any money left.	**Kam mbetur pa para.** [kam mbétuɾ pa pará]

I've lost my ...	**Humba ...** [húmba ...]
Someone stole my ...	**Dikush më vodhi ...** [dikúʃ mə vóði ...]
passport	**pasaportën** [pasapóɾtən]
wallet	**portofol** [poɾtofól]
papers	**dokumentet** [dokuméntɛt]
ticket	**biletën** [bilétən]
money	**para** [pará]
handbag	**çantën** [tʃántən]
camera	**aparatin fotografik** [aparátin fotografík]
laptop	**laptop** [laptóp]
tablet computer	**kompjuterin tabletë** [kompjutérin tablétə]
mobile phone	**celularin** [tsɛlulárin]

Help me!	**Ndihmë!** [ndíhmə!]
What's happened?	**Çfarë ndodhi?** [tʃfárə ndóði?]
fire	**zjarr** [zjar]
shooting	**të shtëna** [tə ʃténa]

murder	**vrasje** [vrásjɛ]
explosion	**shpërthim** [ʃpərθím]
fight	**përleshje** [pərléʃjɛ]

Call the police!	**Thërrisni policinë!** [θərrísni politsínə!]
Please hurry up!	**Ju lutem nxitoni!** [ju lútɛm ndzitóni!]
I'm looking for the police station.	**Kërkoj komisariatin e policisë.** [kərkój komisariátin ɛ politsísə]
I need to make a call.	**Duhet të bëj një telefonatë.** [dúhɛt tə bəj ɲə tɛlɛfonátə]
May I use your phone?	**Mund të përdor telefonin tuaj?** [mund tə pərdór tɛlɛfónin túaj?]

I've been ...	**Më ...** [mə ...]
mugged	**sulmuan** [sulmúan]
robbed	**grabitën** [grabítən]
raped	**përdhunuan** [pərðunúan]
attacked (beaten up)	**rrahën** [ráhən]

Are you all right?	**Jeni mirë?** [jéni mírə?]
Did you see who it was?	**E patë kush ishte?** [ɛ pátə kuʃ íʃtɛ?]
Would you be able to recognize the person?	**Mund ta identifikoni personin?** [mund ta idɛntifikóni pɛrsónin?]
Are you sure?	**Jeni i /e/ sigurt?** [jéni i /ɛ/ sígurt?]

Please calm down.	**Ju lutem qetësohuni.** [ju lútɛm cɛtəsóhuni]
Take it easy!	**Merreni me qetësi!** [mérɛni mɛ cɛtəsí!]
Don't worry!	**Mos u shqetësoni!** [mos u ʃcɛtəsóni!]
Everything will be fine.	**Çdo gjë do rregullohet.** [tʃdo ɟə do rrɛgułóhɛt]
Everything's all right.	**Çdo gjë është në rregull.** [tʃdo ɟə éʃtə nə réguł]
Come here, please.	**ejani këtu, ju lutem.** [éjani kətú], [ju lútɛm]
I have some questions for you.	**Kam disa pyetje për ju.** [kam dísa pýɛtjɛ pər ju]

Wait a moment, please.

Prisni pak, ju lutem.
[prísni pak], [ju lútɛm]

Do you have any I.D.?

A keni ndonjë dokument identifikimi?
[a kéni ndóɲə dokumént idɛntifikími?]

Thanks. You can leave now.

Faleminderit. Mund të largoheni.
[falɛmindérit. mund tə largóhɛni.]

Hands behind your head!

Duart prapa kokës!
[dúart prápa kókəs!]

You're under arrest!

Jeni i /e/ arrestuar!
[jéni i /ɛ/ arɛstúar!]

Health problems

Please help me.	**Ju lutem më ndihmoni.** [ju lútɛm mə ndihmóni]
I don't feel well.	**Nuk ndihem mirë.** [nuk ndíhɛm mírə]
My husband doesn't feel well.	**Burri im nuk ndjehet mirë.** [búri im nuk ndjéhɛt mírə]
My son ...	**Djali im ...** [djáli im ...]
My father ...	**Babai im ...** [babái im ...]
My wife doesn't feel well.	**Gruaja ime nuk ndihet mirë.** [grúaja ímɛ nuk ndíhɛt mírə]
My daughter ...	**Vajza ime ...** [vájza ímɛ ...]
My mother ...	**Nëna ime ...** [nə́na ímɛ ...]
I've got a ...	**Kam ...** [kam ...]
headache	**dhimbje koke** [ðímbjɛ kókɛ]
sore throat	**dhimbje fyti** [ðímbjɛ fýti]
stomach ache	**dhimbje stomaku** [ðímbjɛ stomáku]
toothache	**dhimbje dhëmbi** [ðímbjɛ ðə́mbi]
I feel dizzy.	**Ndjehem i /e/ trullosur.** [ndjéhɛm i /ɛ/ truɬósur]
He has a fever.	**Ka ethe.** [ka éθɛ]
She has a fever.	**Ajo ka ethe.** [ajó ka éθɛ]
I can't breathe.	**Nuk marr dot frymë.** [nuk mar dot frýmə]
I'm short of breath.	**Mbeta pa frymë.** [mbéta pa frýmə]
I am asthmatic.	**unë jam astmatik.** [únə jam astmatík]
I am diabetic.	**Jam me diabet.** [jam mɛ diabét]

I can't sleep.	**Nuk fle dot.** [nuk flɛ dot]
food poisoning	**helmim nga ushqimi** [hɛlmím ŋa uʃcími]

It hurts here.	**Më dhemb këtu.** [mə ðɛmb kətú]
Help me!	**Ndihmë!** [ndíhmə!]
I am here!	**Jam këtu!** [jam kətú!]
We are here!	**Jemi këtu!** [jémi kətú!]
Get me out of here!	**Më nxirrni nga këtu!** [mə ndzírni ŋa kətú!]
I need a doctor.	**Kam nevojë për doktor.** [kam nɛvójə pər doktór]
I can't move.	**Nuk lëviz dot.** [nuk ləvíz dot]
I can't move my legs.	**Nuk lëviz dot këmbët.** [nuk ləvíz dot kə́mbət]

I have a wound.	**Jam plagosur.** [jam plagósur]
Is it serious?	**A është serioze?** [a ə́ʃtə sɛriózɛ?]
My documents are in my pocket.	**Dokumentet e mia janë në xhep.** [dokuméntɛt ɛ mía jánə nə dʒép]
Calm down!	**Qetësohuni!** [cɛtəsóhuni!]
May I use your phone?	**Mund të përdor telefonin tuaj?** [mund tə pərdór tɛlɛfónin túaj?]

Call an ambulance!	**Thërrisni një ambulancë!** [θərísni ɲə ambulántsə!]
It's urgent!	**Është urgjente!** [ə́ʃtə urɟéntɛ!]
It's an emergency!	**Është rast urgjent!** [ə́ʃtə rast urɟént!]
Please hurry up!	**Ju lutem nxitoni!** [ju lútɛm ndzitóni!]
Would you please call a doctor?	**Mund të thërrisni një doktor, ju lutem?** [mund tə θərísni ɲə doktór], [ju lútɛm?]
Where is the hospital?	**Ku është spitali?** [ku ə́ʃtə spitáli?]

How are you feeling?	**Si ndiheni?** [si ndíhɛni?]
Are you all right?	**Jeni mirë?** [jéni mírə?]
What's happened?	**Çfarë ndodhi?** [tʃfárə ndóði?]

I feel better now.	**Ndihem më mirë tani.** [ndíhɛm mə míre taní]
It's OK.	**Është në rregull.** [ə́ʃtə nə régut]
It's all right.	**Është në rregull.** [ə́ʃtə nə régut]

At the pharmacy

pharmacy (drugstore)	**farmaci** [farmatsí]
24-hour pharmacy	**farmaci 24 orë** [farmatsí nəzét ɛ kátər orə]
Where is the closest pharmacy?	**Ku është farmacia më e afërt?** [ku éʃtə farmatsía mə ɛ áfərt?]

Is it open now?	**Është e hapur tani?** [éʃtə ɛ hápur taní?]
At what time does it open?	**Në çfarë ore hapet?** [nə tʃfárə órɛ hápɛt?]
At what time does it close?	**Në çfarë ore mbyllet?** [nə tʃfárə órɛ mbýɫɛt?]

Is it far?	**Është larg?** [éʃtə larg?]
Can I get there on foot?	**Mund të shkoj me këmbë deri atje?** [mund tə ʃkoj mɛ kəmbə déri atjé?]
Can you show me on the map?	**Mund të më tregoni në hartë?** [mund tə mə trɛgóni nə hártə?]

Please give me something for ...	**Ju lutem më jepni diçka për ...** [ju lútɛm mə jépni ditʃká pər ...]
a headache	**dhimbje koke** [ðímbjɛ kókɛ]
a cough	**kollë** [kóɫə]
a cold	**ftohje** [ftóhjɛ]
the flu	**grip** [grip]

a fever	**ethe** [éθɛ]
a stomach ache	**dhimbje stomaku** [ðímbjɛ stomáku]
nausea	**të përziera** [tə pərzíɛra]
diarrhea	**diarre** [diaré]
constipation	**kapsllëk** [kapsɫék]
pain in the back	**dhimbje në shpinë** [ðímbjɛ nə ʃpínə]

chest pain	**dhimbje në kraharor** [ðímbjɛ nə kraharór]
side stitch	**dhimbje në brinjë** [ðímbjɛ nə bríɲə]
abdominal pain	**dhimbje barku** [ðímbjɛ bárku]

pill	**pilulë** [pilúlə]
ointment, cream	**vaj, krem** [vaj], [krɛm]
syrup	**shurup** [ʃurúp]
spray	**sprej** [sprɛj]
drops	**pika** [píka]

You need to go to the hospital.	**Duhet të shkoni në spital.** [dúhɛt tə ʃkóni nə spitál]
health insurance	**sigurim shëndetësor** [sigurím ʃəndɛtəsór]
prescription	**recetë** [rɛtsétə]
insect repellant	**mbrojtës nga insektet** [mbrójtəs ŋa inséktɛt]
Band Aid	**leukoplast** [lɛukoplást]

The bare minimum

Excuse me, ...	**Më falni, ...** [mə fálni, ...]
Hello.	**Përshëndetje.** [pərʃəndétjɛ]
Thank you.	**Faleminderit.** [falɛmindérit]
Good bye.	**Mirupafshim.** [mirupáfʃim]
Yes.	**Po.** [po]
No.	**Jo.** [jo]
I don't know.	**Nuk e di.** [nuk ɛ di]
Where? | Where to? | When?	**Ku? | Për ku? | Kur?** [ku? | pər ku? | kur?]

I need ...	**Më nevojitet ...** [mə nɛvojítɛt ...]
I want ...	**Dua ...** [dúa ...]
Do you have ...?	**Keni ...?** [kéni ...?]
Is there a ... here?	**A ka ... këtu?** [a ka ... kətú?]
May I ...?	**Mund të ...?** [mund tə ...?]
..., please (polite request)	**..., ju lutem** [...], [ju lútɛm]

I'm looking for ...	**Kërkoj ...** [kərkój ...]
the restroom	**tualet** [tualét]
an ATM	**bankomat** [bankomát]
a pharmacy (drugstore)	**farmaci** [farmatsí]
a hospital	**spital** [spitál]
the police station	**komisariat policie** [komisariát politsíɛ]
the subway	**metro** [mɛtró]

a taxi	**taksi** [táksi]
the train station	**stacion treni** [statsión trɛni]

My name is ...	**Më quajnë ...** [mə cúajnə ...]
What's your name?	**Si quheni?** [si cúhɛni?]
Could you please help me?	**Ju lutem, mund të ndihmoni?** [ju lútɛm], [mund tə ndihmóni?]
I've got a problem.	**Kam një problem.** [kam ɲə problém]
I don't feel well.	**Nuk ndihem mirë.** [nuk ndíhɛm mírə]
Call an ambulance!	**Thërrisni një ambulancë!** [θərísni ɲə ambulántsə!]
May I make a call?	**Mund të bëj një telefonatë?** [mund tə bəj ɲə tɛlɛfonátə?]

I'm sorry.	**Më vjen keq.** [mə vjɛn kɛc]
You're welcome.	**Ju lutem.** [ju lútɛm]

I, me	**unë, mua** [únə], [múa]
you (inform.)	**ti** [ti]
he	**ai** [ai]
she	**ajo** [ajó]
they (masc.)	**ata** [atá]
they (fem.)	**ato** [ató]
we	**ne** [nɛ]
you (pl)	**ju** [ju]
you (sg, form.)	**ju** [ju]

ENTRANCE	**HYRJE** [hýrjɛ]
EXIT	**DALJE** [dáljɛ]
OUT OF ORDER	**NUK FUNKSIONON** [nuk funksionón]
CLOSED	**MBYLLUR** [mbýɫur]

OPEN **HAPUR**
[hápur]

FOR WOMEN **PËR FEMRA**
[pər fémra]

FOR MEN **PËR MESHKUJ**
[pər méʃkuj]

MINI DICTIONARY

This section contains 250 useful words required for everyday communication. You will find the names of months and days of the week here. The dictionary also contains topics such as colors, measurements, family, and more

T&P Books Publishing

DICTIONARY CONTENTS

T&P Books Publishing

time	**kohë** (f)	[kóhə]
hour	**orë** (f)	[órə]
half an hour	**gjysmë ore** (f)	[ɟýsmə órɛ]
minute	**minutë** (f)	[minútə]
second	**sekondë** (f)	[sɛkóndə]

today (adv)	**sot**	[sot]
tomorrow (adv)	**nesër**	[nésər]
yesterday (adv)	**dje**	[djé]

Monday	**E hënë** (f)	[ɛ hénə]
Tuesday	**E martë** (f)	[ɛ mártə]
Wednesday	**E mërkurë** (f)	[ɛ mərkúrə]
Thursday	**E enjte** (f)	[ɛ éɲtɛ]
Friday	**E premte** (f)	[ɛ prémtɛ]
Saturday	**E shtunë** (f)	[ɛ ʃtúnə]
Sunday	**E dielë** (f)	[ɛ díɛlə]

day	**ditë** (f)	[dítə]
working day	**ditë pune** (f)	[dítə púnɛ]
public holiday	**festë kombëtare** (f)	[féstə kombətárɛ]
weekend	**fundjavë** (f)	[fundjávə]

week	**javë** (f)	[jávə]
last week (adv)	**javën e kaluar**	[jávən ɛ kalúar]
next week (adv)	**javën e ardhshme**	[jávən ɛ árðʃmɛ]

in the morning	**në mëngjes**	[nə mənɟés]
in the afternoon	**pasdite**	[pasdítɛ]

in the evening	**në mbrëmje**	[nə mbrémjɛ]
tonight (this evening)	**sonte në mbrëmje**	[sóntɛ nə mbrəmjɛ]

at night	**natën**	[nátən]
midnight	**mesnatë** (f)	[mɛsnátə]

January	**Janar** (m)	[janár]
February	**Shkurt** (m)	[ʃkurt]
March	**Mars** (m)	[mars]
April	**Prill** (m)	[priɫ]
May	**Maj** (m)	[maj]
June	**Qershor** (m)	[cɛrʃór]

July	**Korrik** (m)	[korík]
August	**Gusht** (m)	[guʃt]

September	Shtator (m)	[ʃtatór]
October	Tetor (m)	[tɛtór]
November	Nëntor (m)	[nəntór]
December	Dhjetor (m)	[ðjɛtór]

in spring	në pranverë	[nə pranvérə]
in summer	në verë	[nə vérə]
in fall	në vjeshtë	[nə vjéʃtə]
in winter	në dimër	[nə dímər]

month	muaj (m)	[múaj]
season (summer, etc.)	stinë (f)	[stínə]
year	vit (m)	[vit]

2. Numbers. Numerals

0 zero	zero	[zéro]
1 one	një	[ɲə]
2 two	dy	[dy]
3 three	tre	[trɛ]
4 four	katër	[kátər]

5 five	pesë	[pésə]
6 six	gjashtë	[ɟáʃtə]
7 seven	shtatë	[ʃtátə]
8 eight	tetë	[tétə]
9 nine	nëntë	[nəntə]
10 ten	dhjetë	[ðjétə]

11 eleven	njëmbëdhjetë	[ɲəmbəðjétə]
12 twelve	dymbëdhjetë	[dymbəðjétə]
13 thirteen	trembëdhjetë	[trɛmbəðjétə]
14 fourteen	katërmbëdhjetë	[katərmbəðjétə]
15 fifteen	pesëmbëdhjetë	[pɛsəmbəðjétə]

16 sixteen	gjashtëmbëdhjetë	[ɟaʃtəmbəðjétə]
17 seventeen	shtatëmbëdhjetë	[ʃtatəmbəðjétə]
18 eighteen	tetëmbëdhjetë	[tɛtəmbəðjétə]
19 nineteen	nëntëmbëdhjetë	[nəntəmbəðjétə]

20 twenty	njëzet	[ɲəzét]
30 thirty	tridhjetë	[triðjétə]
40 forty	dyzet	[dyzét]
50 fifty	pesëdhjetë	[pɛsəðjétə]

60 sixty	gjashtëdhjetë	[ɟaʃtəðjétə]
70 seventy	shtatëdhjetë	[ʃtatəðjétə]
80 eighty	tetëdhjetë	[tɛtəðjétə]
90 ninety	nëntëdhjetë	[nəntəðjétə]
100 one hundred	njëqind	[ɲəcínd]

200 two hundred	dyqind	[dycínd]
300 three hundred	treqind	[trɛcínd]
400 four hundred	katërqind	[katərcínd]
500 five hundred	pesëqind	[pɛsəcínd]

600 six hundred	gjashtëqind	[ɟaʃtəcínd]
700 seven hundred	shtatëqind	[ʃtatəcínd]
800 eight hundred	tetëqind	[tɛtəcínd]
900 nine hundred	nëntëqind	[nəntəcínd]
1000 one thousand	një mijë	[ɲə míjə]

| 10000 ten thousand | dhjetë mijë | [ðjétə míjə] |
| one hundred thousand | njëqind mijë | [ɲəcínd míjə] |

| million | milion (m) | [milión] |
| billion | miliardë (f) | [miliárdə] |

3. Humans. Family

man (adult male)	burrë (m)	[búrə]
young man	djalë i ri (m)	[djálə i rí]
woman	grua (f)	[grúa]
girl (young woman)	vajzë (f)	[vájzə]
old man	plak (m)	[plak]
old woman	plakë (f)	[plákə]

mother	nënë (f)	[nénə]
father	baba (f)	[babá]
son	bir (m)	[bir]
daughter	bijë (f)	[bíjə]
brother	vëlla (m)	[vəłá]
sister	motër (f)	[mótər]

parents	prindër (pl)	[príndər]
child	fëmijë (f)	[fəmíjə]
children	fëmijë (pl)	[fəmíjə]
stepmother	njerkë (f)	[nérkə]
stepfather	njerk (m)	[nérk]

grandmother	gjyshe (f)	[ɟýʃɛ]
grandfather	gjysh (m)	[ɟyʃ]
grandson	nip (m)	[nip]
granddaughter	mbesë (f)	[mbésə]
grandchildren	nipër e mbesa (pl)	[nípər ɛ mbésa]

uncle	dajë (f)	[dájə]
aunt	teze (f)	[tézɛ]
nephew	nip (m)	[nip]
niece	mbesë (f)	[mbésə]
wife	bashkëshorte (f)	[baʃkəʃórtɛ]

husband	bashkëshort (m)	[baʃkəʃórt]
married (masc.)	i martuar	[i martúar]
married (fem.)	e martuar	[ɛ martúar]
widow	vejushë (f)	[vɛjúʃə]
widower	vejan (m)	[vɛján]

| name (first name) | emër (m) | [émər] |
| surname (last name) | mbiemër (m) | [mbiémər] |

relative	kushëri (m)	[kuʃərí]
friend (masc.)	mik (m)	[mik]
friendship	miqësi (f)	[micəsí]

partner	partner (m)	[partnér]
superior (n)	epror (m)	[ɛprór]
colleague	koleg (m)	[kolég]
neighbors	komshinj (pl)	[komʃíɲ]

4. Human body

body	trup (m)	[trup]
heart	zemër (f)	[zémər]
blood	gjak (m)	[ɟak]
brain	tru (m)	[tru]

bone	kockë (f)	[kótskə]
spine (backbone)	shtyllë kurrizore (f)	[ʃtɨɫə kurizórɛ]
rib	brinjë (f)	[bríɲə]
lungs	mushkëri (m)	[muʃkərí]
skin	lëkurë (f)	[ləkúrə]

head	kokë (f)	[kókə]
face	fytyrë (f)	[fytɨrə]
nose	hundë (f)	[húndə]
forehead	ball (m)	[báɫ]
cheek	faqe (f)	[fácɛ]

mouth	gojë (f)	[gójə]
tongue	gjuhë (f)	[ɟúhə]
tooth	dhëmb (m)	[ðəmb]
lips	buzë (f)	[búzə]
chin	mjekër (f)	[mjékər]

ear	vesh (m)	[vɛʃ]
neck	qafë (f)	[cáfə]
eye	sy (m)	[sy]
pupil	bebëz (f)	[bébəz]
eyebrow	vetull (f)	[vétuɫ]
eyelash	qerpik (m)	[cɛrpík]
hair	flokë (pl)	[flókə]

hairstyle	model flokësh (m)	[modél flókəʃ]
mustache	mustaqe (f)	[mustácɛ]
beard	mjekër (f)	[mjékər]
to have (a beard, etc.)	lë mjekër	[lə mjékər]
bald (adj)	qeros	[cɛrós]

hand	dorë (f)	[dórə]
arm	krah (m)	[krah]
finger	gisht i dorës (m)	[gíʃt i dórəs]
nail	thua (f)	[θúa]
palm	pëllëmbë dore (f)	[pəłəmbə dórɛ]

shoulder	shpatull (f)	[ʃpátuł]
leg	këmbë (f)	[kémbə]
knee	gju (m)	[ɟú]
heel	thembër (f)	[θémbər]
back	kurriz (m)	[kuríz]

5. Clothing. Personal accessories

clothes	rroba (f)	[róba]
coat (overcoat)	pallto (f)	[páłto]
fur coat	gëzof (m)	[gəzóf]
jacket (e.g., leather ~)	xhaketë (f)	[dʒakétə]
raincoat (trenchcoat, etc.)	pardesy (f)	[pardɛsý]

shirt (button shirt)	këmishë (f)	[kəmíʃə]
pants	pantallona (f)	[pantałóna]
suit jacket	xhaketë kostumi (f)	[dʒakétə kostúmi]
suit	kostum (m)	[kostúm]

dress (frock)	fustan (m)	[fustán]
skirt	fund (m)	[fund]
T-shirt	bluzë (f)	[blúzə]
bathrobe	peshqir trupi (m)	[pɛʃcír trúpi]
pajamas	pizhame (f)	[piʒámɛ]
workwear	rroba pune (f)	[róba púnɛ]

underwear	të brendshme (f)	[tə bréndʃmɛ]
socks	çorape (pl)	[tʃorápɛ]
bra	sytjena (f)	[sytjéna]
pantyhose	geta (f)	[géta]
stockings (thigh highs)	çorape të holla (pl)	[tʃorápɛ tə hóła]
bathing suit	rrobë banje (f)	[róbə báɲɛ]

hat	kapelë (f)	[kapélə]
footwear	këpucë (pl)	[kəpútsə]
boots (e.g., cowboy ~)	çizme (pl)	[tʃízmɛ]
heel	takë (f)	[tákə]
shoestring	lidhëse këpucësh (f)	[líðəsɛ kəpútsəʃ]

shoe polish	**bojë këpucësh** (f)	[bójə kəpútsəʃ]
gloves	**dorëza** (pl)	[dórəza]
mittens	**doreza** (f)	[doréza]
scarf (muffler)	**shall** (m)	[ʃaɫ]
glasses (eyeglasses)	**syze** (f)	[sýzɛ]
umbrella	**çadër** (f)	[tʃádər]
tie (necktie)	**kravatë** (f)	[kravátə]
handkerchief	**shami** (f)	[ʃamí]
comb	**krehër** (m)	[kréhər]
hairbrush	**furçë flokësh** (f)	[fúrtʃə flókəʃ]
buckle	**tokëz** (f)	[tókəz]
belt	**rrip** (m)	[rip]
purse	**çantë** (f)	[tʃántə]

6. House. Apartment

apartment	**apartament** (m)	[apartamént]
room	**dhomë** (f)	[ðómə]
bedroom	**dhomë gjumi** (f)	[ðómə ɟúmi]
dining room	**dhomë ngrënie** (f)	[ðómə ŋrəníɛ]
living room	**dhomë ndeje** (f)	[ðómə ndéjɛ]
study (home office)	**dhomë pune** (f)	[ðómə púnɛ]
entry room	**hyrje** (f)	[hýrjɛ]
bathroom (room with a bath or shower)	**banjo** (f)	[báɲo]
half bath	**tualet** (m)	[tualét]
vacuum cleaner	**fshesë elektrike** (f)	[fʃésə ɛlɛktríkɛ]
mop	**shtupë** (f)	[ʃtúpə]
dust cloth	**leckë** (f)	[létskə]
short broom	**fshesë** (f)	[fʃésə]
dustpan	**kaci** (f)	[katsí]
furniture	**orendi** (f)	[orɛndí]
table	**tryezë** (f)	[tryézə]
chair	**karrige** (f)	[karígɛ]
armchair	**kolltuk** (m)	[koɫtúk]
mirror	**pasqyrë** (f)	[pascýrə]
carpet	**qilim** (m)	[cilím]
fireplace	**oxhak** (m)	[odʒák]
drapes	**perde** (f)	[pérdɛ]
table lamp	**llambë tavoline** (f)	[ɫámbə tavolínɛ]
chandelier	**llambadar** (m)	[ɫambadár]
kitchen	**kuzhinë** (f)	[kuʒínə]
gas stove (range)	**sobë me gaz** (f)	[sóbə mɛ gaz]

electric stove	sobë elektrike (f)	[sóbə ɛlɛktríkɛ]
microwave oven	mikrovalë (f)	[mikroválə]
refrigerator	frigorifer (m)	[frigorifér]
freezer	frigorifer (m)	[frigorifér]
dishwasher	pjatalarëse (f)	[pjatalárəsɛ]
faucet	rubinet (m)	[rubinét]
meat grinder	grirëse mishi (f)	[grírəsɛ míʃi]
juicer	shtrydhëse frutash (f)	[ʃtrýðəsɛ frútaʃ]
toaster	toster (m)	[tostér]
mixer	mikser (m)	[miksér]
coffee machine	makinë kafeje (f)	[makínə kaféjɛ]
kettle	çajnik (m)	[tʃajník]
teapot	çajnik (m)	[tʃajník]
TV set	televizor (m)	[tɛlɛvizór]
VCR (video recorder)	video regjistrues (m)	[vídɛo rɟistrúɛs]
iron (e.g., steam ~)	hekur (m)	[hékur]
telephone	telefon (m)	[tɛlɛfón]

CPSIA information can be obtained
at www.ICGtesting.com
Printed in the USA
BVHW042212060219
539690BV00012B/175/P